BONDAGE
TO BLESSING

Sorrey L. Mitchell

BONDAGE
TO BLESSING

A SPIRITUAL GUIDE TO FINANCES IN THE END TIMES

JERRY MITCHELL

WinePressPublishing
Great Books, Defined.

WinePress Publishing (PO Box 428, Enumclaw, WA 98022) functions only as book publisher. As such, the ultimate design, content, editorial accuracy, and views expressed or implied in this work are those of the author.

Unless otherwise noted, all Scriptures are taken from the *New American Standard Bible*®, Copyright © 1960, 1962, 1963, 1968, 1971, 1972, 1973, 1975, 1977, 1995 by The Lockman Foundation. Used by permission.

Scripture references marked KJV are taken from the *King James Version* of the Bible, 1987 printing.

Scripture references marked NKJV are taken from the *New King James Version*. Copyright © 1982 by Thomas Nelson, Inc. Used by permission. All rights reserved.

ISBN 13: 978-1-4141-2380-6
ISBN 10: 1-4141-2380-9
Library of Congress Catalog Card Number: 2012909220

CONTENTS

FOREWORD

BY ROBYN McCRIGHT

IN A WORLD of hard economic times and money woes, this book comes at an excellent time. There are many "how to" books on finances, both secular and Christian. In my own life, I have read and attended workshops on how to manage money and get out of debt, but have struggled and given up when things didn't work out as they were supposed to. It's true that you have to follow the plan laid out and stay consistent, but often I found that following the plan, even the Christian plan, just didn't seem to pan out as well as it should. I felt no hope or joy. The constant struggle seemed monotonous and draining instead of freeing and abundant as I thought it would be if I was doing it God's way. This book brings out the key point that many Christians miss when it comes to having financial freedom.

This is not just another "how to" book. Jerry shares biblical insight on what God says about money, but goes on to share the missing link that we need to have financial freedom and abundance, not just in our financial affairs, but in every area of our lives.

If you've been through many financial courses and haven't had it work out well, or you are deep in debt, then let this book encourage you as you read it and find the key that so many Christians miss. This book offers fresh insight on what God says in the Bible in order to lead each of us to a life of financial deliverance and abundance. Come experience the joy!

ACKNOWLEDGMENTS

I'D LIKE TO give a big thank you to my wife, Karen, for her support and encouragement. Without her, publishing this book would not have happened.

Karen, I love you with all my heart.

CHAPTER 1

FINANCIAL PRINCIPLES

After years of careful Bible study and twenty five years of being in the financial world I have concluded that the financial principles found in the Bible directly oppose those taught by the world.

DO YOU BELIEVE that? It's true. The fact is that most of God's people do not know that the financial principles in the Bible are different from those taught by so-called financial experts. Many of the books that purport to teach Christian finance are, in reality, only attempts to "Christianize" teachings taken from the world. Biblical truths about finance deal with the heart and point very quickly to one's relationship with God Himself.

The good news is this: there are guidelines in the Bible about how to manage the finances God puts in our hands.

Our lives are filled with instruction about managing money. Parents begin very early to teach their children about it—what it is and what it's used for. Children learn quickly that money is a valuable possession. They learn that with money they can buy the things they want. They learn that every human desire can be satisfied if you only have money. They learn that people with money get their way. Money brings power—with money, you can be whoever you want to be.

As they absorb all these lessons taught by both words and example, children learn that to get money is one of the top priorities of life. It is a rude awakening, however, to discover that one must work to obtain money, therefore ushering in a whole new phase of a child's education about money. Now enter the motivators! They have learned that if you only want money bad enough, you can have it. With the proper discipline, education, and work ethic, you can become rich.

Through this bombardment of information and instruction, people take into their hearts principles about finance from the world. They learn that it is good to desire things. They learn that money is one of the most important things in life, and for many, it is the *most* important thing. They learn that to obtain money is to be successful. They learn that to have good credit and use debt is desirable, and in fact, prestigious. They learn that people without money are not good, and people with money are good. They learn that it is proper to dedicate all of one's time and energy to obtain money.

They also learn they *own* money—and this belief is the most damaging of all the principles people learn from the world. The world at large passes on the entitlement belief that people should have a sense of ownership in their heart about money and all of their possessions. This sense of ownership transcends all other financial principles. What money a person earns in the pursuit of money is his (or hers) and his alone. He can do with it what he pleases.

The church makes a good attempt to teach new converts that the principles they have learned from the world are wrong. A new Christian begins an exciting new adventure as he learns to replace hate with love, and sadness with joy. A whole new vocabulary opens up as the new Christian learns to lay aside profanity and curses for language more befitting a Christian. He learns to spend his time seeking God's face instead of worldly pleasures. He learns that almost all things of importance and priority in life are different from what the world taught him—all except money. Very few if any ever tells the new believer that the principles he has taken so deeply into his heart about money are wrong and God has a much better way.

Christians learn that their mind, body, talents, time, and energy all belong to God. God has bought them with a price, the precious blood of Jesus. But the church often leaves the Christian's sense of ownership of his or her money untouched. The end result is a Christian who believes he belongs to God, but his money belongs to him. The church teaches that the tithe belongs to God and leaves the Christian with the strong implication that the ninety percent left is his to do with as he pleases.

Thus, the Christian's sense of ownership remains intact in his heart, along with the other financial principles of the world, left to cause havoc with his relationship with God. Principles from the world left unchanged in the Christian heart have the power to rise up and turn the Christian away from the Lord.

But those who want to get rich fall into temptation and a snare and many foolish and harmful desires which plunge men into ruin and destruction. For the love of money is a root of all sorts of evil, and some by longing for it have wandered away from the faith and pierced themselves with many griefs. But flee from these things, you man of God, and pursue righteousness, godliness, faith, love, perseverance and gentleness.

—1 Timothy 6:9-11

The financial principles of the world set up the heart to love money. They instill a deep longing for money, an insatiable desire to be rich. Christians who have not allowed God to change their hearts about these things find themselves in the middle of many temptations—or in modern terms, "snares or traps, foolish and harmful desires." Allowing these evils in the Christian heart will eventually damage our close relationship with God.

The nation of Israel in the Old Testament is our example: "Now these things happened as examples for us, so that we would not crave evil things as they also craved" (1 Cor. 10:6). Israel as a nation is a symbol of each Christian. We can compare the behavior of the whole nation of Israel coming out of Egypt and crossing the Red Sea with that of each individual Christian and his journey of coming into Christ by faith.

The apostle Paul in 1 Corinthians 10:1-4 wrote:

For I do not want you to be unaware, brethren, that our fathers were all under the cloud and all passed through the sea; and all were baptized into Moses in the cloud and in the sea; and all ate the same spiritual food; and all drank the same spiritual drink, for they were drinking form a spiritual rock which followed them; and the rock was Christ.

The nation of Israel came out of Egypt by way of the Red Sea into God, just as we came out of the world into God through the red blood of Jesus. Read Exodus 14 and see how beautifully Israel's crossing of the Red Sea pictures salvation. Israel's first experience in God was wandering in the wilderness for forty years.

God explained His purpose for those forty years in Deuteronomy 8. He tested them in order to know what was in their heart, to humble them, and to teach them that man does not live by bread alone, but by everything that proceeds out of the mouth of the Lord. Their clothes did not wear out; their feet did not swell. God fed them with manna, and He gave them water from a rock. The wilderness was God's time to teach them to trust the Lord for everything, to listen intently for His voice, and be careful to do all that He said. It was to prepare them to go into the Promised Land, where there was great blessing and great prosperity awaiting them.

There is a wilderness for each Christian. In the beginning of that wilderness, God invites each of us into His presence. In Exodus 19:3-6, God invited Israel into His presence, every person. God wanted Israel to be a kingdom of priests coming into His presence and getting to know Him face to face. Sadly, only Moses, Aaron, Joshua, Caleb, and seventy of the elders were willing to meet with God on the mountain (Exodus 24:9-10). It is a beautiful picture to see Moses climbing the mountain, only to disappear into the presence of God. Paul the apostle pointed out that Moses' face was shining as he came out of God's presence, but the shine began to fade (2 Cor. 3:13).

For us today, now that the precious Holy Spirit has taken up residence in our mortal bodies, the shining need not fade, but can get brighter. Israel needed to physically enter God's presence, because only there could He change the attitudes and beliefs Israel had taken into their hearts while in Egypt. Today, Christ gives us access to God's presence where He can change the things taken into our hearts from the world.

Exodus 20:19 tells us that the people of Israel decided in their hearts not to come to God; they wanted to stand at a distance from God. They said, "Let Moses go to God and then come to tell us what He said." The thing that makes this reluctance on their part so sad is that the principles learned in Egypt, which they had taken deep into their hearts, could not be changed while they stood at a distance from God, just as that part of us that will not come to God must die before we can enter His rest. Israel chose to die in the wilderness by not coming into God's presence. It took forty years, but the people could not enter the Promised Land until that part of them that refused to enter His presence was dead. During the forty years of wandering in the wilderness, part of Israel was dying while the other part was learning to depend on God for everything.

So it is with us. That which we have learned from the world and taken into our heart must die, and a new part of us must grow up that is willing to walk in His presence. We must unlearn all the principles of the world and learn the principles He teaches us that the Holy Spirit administers in the pages of His Word.

The financial principles that we must learn in our wilderness are the very same ones the people of Israel learned in their wilderness. The wealth they brought from Egypt was of no value in the wilderness. There were no stores or shopping centers in the wilderness. Wealth brought from Egypt was only excess baggage to be carried along in the wilderness. Its only value was to make a golden calf for them to worship, thereby sinning against God.

In the wilderness, all of the provisions to support life came from God. God gave His people food, water, and clothing for forty years. They were free from disease; their feet did not even swell. God protected them from any and all who would be their enemy. God stood over them in a cloud by day, protecting them from the heat, and a pillar of fire by night, protecting them from the cold.

Through all of these provisions, they learned that God was their source. In the wilderness, they could do nothing to provide for themselves. Nothing would grow in the wilderness. They had to trust God to be their provider. Only after the forty years ended did they realize the magnitude of God's provision.

Similarly for us, the wilderness is that time in our lives when we are not aware that God is involved in our lives at all. During wilderness times, Christians only wish God would get involved in their lives, but they do not believe God is near to them or even cares. Though He is there, they often don't recognize His presence or provision.

When a Christian is set free and enters the abundant life, the Spirit-filled life, the believer then realizes, as he or she looks back, that God involved Himself in every little detail and miraculously provided for every need. In His wilderness experience, Jesus quotes a verse from Deuteronomy 8:3 to Satan: "Man does not live by bread alone, but man lives by everything that proceeds out of the mouth of the LORD." God sends each of us to the wilderness, where we learn to trust Him because we have to. This becomes our training ground to prepare us for the Promised Land, where everything we touch is blessed and prospers. In that land we must trust Him because we want to, not because we have to.

I believe most Christians' faith in God's provision and protection dies in the wilderness. But for those who will meet with God face to face and let Him take the world out of them and change them into the image of His dear Son, there is a Promised Land flowing with milk and honey.

It is so important to have biblical principles seated deep in our hearts. In the Jewish faith, many parents throughout the centuries have taught—and still teach today—their children from an early age that they are special to God. They teach them that God will bless them because they are beloved, so they live with an expectation of good financial success.

They also believe what is theirs actually belongs to all Israel, so they are very willing to give their wealth, just as they were when they had a chance to establish a new nation of Israel in 1948. They also help each other because they feel they are a part of Israel as a whole. They believe they should live out of a humble portion of their income, and out of every dollar they earn, they are to keep or invest a portion for the accumulation of wealth. These principles have served them well. In virtually every free nation in the world, Jewish citizens have accumulated great wealth and risen to power and influence.

We can learn from their examples, and these principles, for the most part, come from the Old Testament. Israel as a whole does not accept Jesus as Messiah, so they do not teach from the New Testament. Even so, these principles have their foundation in the Bible and they have worked wonderfully.

Should not we, who know Jesus and have the leading of the Holy Spirit, do as well, or even better? We must allow God to build in us these underlying principles that control our financial thinking and behavior.

CHAPTER 2

PREPARATION

I have learned to be content in whatever circumstances I am.
—Philippians 4:11

ARE YOU PREPARED to enter the Promised Land? Just as Israel had to prepare to enter their Promised Land, we must also prepare for ours.

Israel eventually came to the east bank of the Jordan after the last unbeliever had died. They camped there long enough to reflect on the lessons learned in the wilderness. They knew they must change leaders—Moses must die and Joshua would take command. This realization was a turning point for them.

We, too, have a turning point. Ours is from law to grace, when we turn from obeying rules religiously to a relationship with the Holy Spirit, whereby we listen to every word He speaks and learn to follow His instruction. It's time for us to spy out the Promised Land. We must learn at what cost our Promised Land is to be taken, and how we are to live once we take it.

Israel needed to know that the tremendous abundance in the land had wicked and pagan caretakers who were, nonetheless, appointed by God Himself. The good of the land and its abundance belonged to Israel, a gift from God, but in their absence, God appointed ungodly nations to develop and protect what they would hand over to Israel in God's good time. Israel would first need to depose and dispossess the ungodly caretakers in order to claim God's gift. This would not be easy. It would involve years of bloody battles fought against vastly overwhelming odds, so that in order to win, they had to have God's help, even as they had God's provision in the wilderness.

The Christian also engages in battle and must turn to God for help. The believer's battles are the spiritual equivalent to Israel's physical battles. God has prepared and put in us many wonderful and perfect gifts, but evil and pagan caretakers have been put in charge. We see that all of the desires that drive our lives, from hunger to sex, from fear to loneliness, from the desire to be alone to the desire to be rich, are wonderful gifts from God, but are controlled by the world, or our past, or some evil taskmaster. The battles to win over this enemy pit us against evil forces far beyond our ability to handle, and without the Holy Spirit's help, we do not win.

It is just as necessary for us to depend on His leadership as it was for Israel. Cleansing of the spiritual landscape is necessary for the Christian to take possession of the abundant life. We must be willing to bring every part of our life into submission to the Lord Jesus and the Holy Spirit, including our finances. For Israel, understanding the commitment and experience of crossing the Jordan to enter the Promised Land meant abandoning themselves to God. It meant committing to follow His leadership into the fulfillment of God's promises to them and all their forefathers. It meant determining to seek God's face and His good pleasure in spite of overwhelming odds against them. Perhaps what provides the greatest temptation to turn away from God is to experience the great blessings in the "Promised Land." Therefore we must be determined to focus on God Himself as our treasure and love only Him.

I believe God desires to bring us to a place in Him where He can bless us with all the wealth of the world and it has no power over our heart. He wants us to be so in love with Him that money offers no distraction. It is true that, in the light of His wonderful face, "the things of this world will grow strangely dim." For the Christian, "crossing the Jordan" represents entering into the abundant life, the Spirit-filled life. It may well begin with what some call the baptism of the Holy Spirit, but it is much more than that. It is life after dying to the self. It is the life that comes after being raised with Jesus, so beautifully pictured in baptism. It is being in touch with the Holy Spirit to the point that we hear His voice continually and consult Him, asking His direction about every step we take and about every attitude of the heart and every thought that passes through our minds.

We Must Understand and Live by the Word of the Lord

In order to live the abundant life, we must learn the things Israel learned while in the wilderness:

- We must learn to live by every word that proceeds out of the mouth of the Lord. We must not assume ownership of our lives, because just as the land Israel was about to enter was holy (it belonged to God), so our lives are holy, belonging to God. If we have assumed ownership in our hearts, we must transfer that ownership back to God. For Israel to live in the Promised Land and for us to live the abundant life, we must see ourselves as God sees us.

• We must understand that God has said the ability to make wealth is in us.

> Deuteronomy 8:18 says, "But thou shalt remember the LORD thy God: for it is he that giveth thee power to get wealth, that he may establish his covenant which he sware unto thy fathers, as it is this day" (KJV).

We must believe He has put within us every quality it takes to make wealth. To be productive in some way and to manage properly what He does put in our care as good stewards of His resources. He wants us to be humble and be content with a humble life style, for He has promised if we do not humble ourselves, He will humble us. We are to be disciplined and live disciplined lives, taking much care and giving the proper attention to every detail. We are to be thankful and full of joy, content in whatever circumstances we find ourselves. Paul explains in Philippians 4:11-12:

> Not that I speak from want, for I have learned to be content in whatever circumstances I am. I know how to get along with humble means, and I also

know how to live in prosperity; in any and every circumstance I have learned the secret of being filled and going hungry, both of having abundance and suffering need.

- We must put others' welfare very high on our priority list. Israel was required to stay together in war until all the land was taken. God did not permit them to settle down in the land given to them until all their brothers had their land secured as well. We must not be selfish in our attitudes, but we must be very responsive to the needs of others.

    Proverbs 19:17 says, "He that hath pity upon the poor lendeth unto the LORD, and that which he hath given will he pay him again" (KJV).

    Think about it. If God asks you to lend Him some money, could you trust Him to repay it? We must have an attitude that our life and everything in it is God's, therefore motivating in us the very highest work ethic and the highest respect for His property because we have the highest respect for Him.

- We must know in our hearts that we are not bound by what we see, but by what God has said in His Word and in our hearts. We must be willing to live on the edge of what we can understand and, from time to time, step over into the supernatural, the realm of miracles. Just as Jesus' life was marked by the miracles, so will ours be. Having learned these lessons, we are now ready to undertake the possession of the Promised Land, the abundant life.

Here is an illustration that applies biblical truth to our world today: Suppose you have a friend whom you trust. You ask him to take charge of some of your resources that you want to go to your children who you love very much. You give him very specific instructions on how and when your children are to receive your provisions, and you think you are crystal clear and that your friend understands your wishes. Your friend accepts the job as trustee of your money and is willing to pass it on to your children. Later, you discover that your children have not been receiving any money and have not been provided for as you intended. You also discover that your friend has been buying houses and cars and things for himself. He obviously has assumed ownership of your money and forgotten about his fiduciary responsibilities as a trustee. How would you feel, and what would you do about the situation and your friend?

We Must Understand We Are Trustees, Not Owners

Malachi 3:8 says, "Will a man rob God? Yet you are robbing Me! But you say, 'How have we robbed You?' In tithes and offerings."

Too often, we who are *trustees* have assumed ownership of the funds that God provided, and used them to increase our so-called standard of living. When we believe we own something, we develop a sense of pride. We feel we can decide what to do with it, and how to treat it. We take offense if someone tries to tell us what to do with it. We believe, due to our training and heritage, that we own our money. We make decisions about money and seek counsel from no one.

Recognizing this attitude is only the first step in repairing the damage. We must allow God to take money out of our hearts. The Holy Spirit is the only One who can do that kind of heart surgery.

Before Israel could possess the Promised Land, they had to win it in battle. We have a battle to win, as well, against our own pagan caretakers before we can possess our Promised Land. The Israelites were under orders from God to destroy every remnant of their enemies. Similarly, we must undertake to totally annihilate the things in us that oppose the abundant life in Christ. Our sense of ownership is just one of these enemies. When we do destroy it, we find that earning money and managing it for our Lord becomes an exciting spiritual experience. Once you are in the Promised Land, see its potential and believe what God has told you about it. Being there becomes a wonderful adventure with Christ and the Holy Spirit.

Second Chronicles 7:14 says, "And My people who are called by My name humble themselves and pray and seek My face and turn from their wicked ways, then I will hear from heaven, will forgive their sin and will heal their land."

Humility flies in the face of human pride. It goes against our human nature. Humility is the opposite of pride. It makes others more important than us. It takes us out of the race to keep up with the Joneses. Humility does not mean one thinks little of himself, but a humble person believes what God has said about him. He is loved supremely by the Creator of the whole universe. He is created in the image of God and recreated after the very likeness of God's Son.

The Christian is filled with the very Spirit that raised Jesus from the dead. A humble person knows he is God's crowning achievement, but he is also aware of how valuable others are. He can see them through the eyes of God, who loved them so much that He gave His Son for them. Humility means to seek first the kingdom of God and let God be the one who determines your station in this life. Humility exalts Jesus, and lets Jesus be the one who exalts you. A humble person is not concerned about living in a fancy home or driving a fancy car. Humility does not try to impress anyone and does not concern itself with impressing others with material possessions.

CHAPTER 3

BEING AN ACTIVE MANAGER

If we confess our sins, He is faithful and righteous to forgive
us our sins and to cleanse us from all unrighteousness.
—1 John 1:9

IT IS SO easy to go with the flow. Our biggest temptation is
to let things slide. When we do this in our finances, we find
ourselves yielding to the things that pressure us the most: impulse
spending, using credit, paying the bills that scream the loudest,
and planning in retrospect. By "planning in retrospect," I mean
planning how we are going to pay money we have already spent;
it is like eating bread that is not yet ours. Most people do their
tax planning when it is time to file the tax return, and that is
planning for the year that has already gone by. We need to change
our view from the past to the future.

Taking control is not easy, but that is what God's Word says
to do. In other areas of our lives, we take control at the Holy

Spirit's prompting. We stop smoking or drinking; we clean up our language and our thought life; we select our friends and how to use our time. Taking control may begin with a commitment, but it also requires continual commitment every day and every time we use our money. Most of the thoughts that pass through our minds involve the spending of money. We must bring those thoughts under our control, submitting them to God's Word and the leading of the Holy Spirit.

Taking control requires first a commitment to find out where we are at this present time, how we got there, and the mistakes made in the past that we need to change. We then repent and ask God to forgive us our debts. He is faithful and just to forgive us of our sins and to cleanse us of all our unrighteousness (1 John 1:9).

We then need to know where we should be. God will reveal this in His Word and through prayer. It will be a picture of us, out of debt, having cash reserves to pay for everything, using credit wisely, giving faithfully, accumulating assets to provide for the future, having resources to give to every good cause, becoming independent so we're not chained to a job to provide for our living, and becoming financially free so that if He chooses, God could lead us to go anywhere and do anything in this world.

Taking control means to change. If we are going to change, we need to know what to change. We need to know what we do as a result of going with the flow. What are some examples of impulse spending? I don't know if any of these examples fit you, but they fit me. A friend suggested I go fishing with him, so I mentioned the invitation to my wife and she thought it would be good for me. I would get a much-needed break and have some good fellowship as well. In fact, we could make a long list of benefits, so it looked like the right thing to do. Problem was, I had no fishing gear. So I went out to buy a rod and reel, only to discover I needed lures, line, a tackle box, and clothing. The more I saw, the more I needed, and the list got bigger and bigger. Then there was the loss of work (not paid), that really took a bite out of our budget. Looking back, it was a very expensive impulse. Don't misunderstand—a fishing trip is not wrong, but spending money on impulse is.

Here is another example: I love my wife very much and want to do really nice things for her. So if she sees a car or something she likes, I will do my best to get it for her. Once she needed a car and saw one she liked, so I bought it and took on payments we really could not afford. Again, trying to please your wife is not wrong; in fact, it is admirable, but buying on impulse is wrong. Other very important things suffered greatly as a result of the long-term effects of that impulse. Of course, we should also not overlook the smaller impulses that happen as a result of shopping trips, or going out to eat, or gift buying.

Most people really do not know where their money goes and may have to keep a written record for two or three months to find out. Taking control of these impulses will take a real effort, discipline, planning, and prayer. It is not easy, as old habits die hard, but it can be done if we are determined and stay at it.

In the beginning, taking control means we must deal with a situation that is far less than perfect. Our planning, of necessity, must deal with past mistakes and focus on the past, but as we gain control, our focus will change gradually to the future. First, we must plan to get out of debt, stop the foolish spending, and start a cash reserve, all at the same time. Eventually, we will plan for long-term future goals such as retirement, college for the kids or perhaps even ourselves, purchase of a house or a farm, and short-term future goals such as vacations, Christmas gifts, remodeling projects, or a new car. Future spending may include investment properties or investment ideas. Think about it: wouldn't it be much more satisfying and rewarding if you knew the past was paid for, the present was under your complete control, and your planning was looking at the future near and far?

If you share the decision-making process—and every married couple should—you need to come into full agreement about taking control. You need to admit mistakes together, communicate effectively, plan and pray together, and see and plan the future together. But please resist the temptation to accuse or blame each other. Frustrations will run high and the temptation to vent these frustrations on the one you love the most will certainly be present; the devil will see to it. After all, it was Satan who brought about the situation you and others may be in, by deception, temptation, and attacks against you and others of God's people. It's what he does; he does not want any of God's people experiencing God's blessings, especially financial ones. He knows our effectiveness is severely hampered when we are in financial bondage.

Taking control is a commitment not to let the enemy of our faith win one more battle. Being wise to his devices and aware of God's promises and instructions give us the power over him, but don't be too hard on yourself or each other when you fail. Just tell the Lord about it, ask His forgiveness, and start again. God has promised that once we are in His Son Jesus Christ, we are destined to be conformed to His image, perfect in every way. So just keep at it. When you fall, get up. When you make a mistake, and you will, start again. One thing about God's people who are in a tight relationship with Him is they just won't quit—so keep on keeping on. Always know that all your relationships—with God, your spouse, children, friends, and everyone else—are far more important than money. Keep the proper perspective; mind money well, but mind your relationships more.

CHAPTER 4

WORK ETHICS

Whether, then, you eat or drink or whatever you do, do all
to the glory of God.

—1 Corinthians 10:31

A S A BOY, I was very fortunate to have parents who instilled
in me a good work ethic. Daddy taught us that we should
do the very best job we could at everything we did. He used to
say, "It's not worth doing if you don't do your best." I grew up
believing that at least part of a man's worth was measured by how
he worked. His work performance went right along with the value
of his word. Daddy also used to say, "If you do your best, you will
be promoted to that level and paid accordingly." We grew up in a
farming and ranching community in Colorado. Hard work was
very necessary for the health of the whole community. It is no
less important now. The Bible teaches that very same work ethic.

Our society today does not promote or teach good work
ethics. I am not opposed to unions. We certainly need them, but

when a job is protected by something other than the quality of one's work, the work ethic begins to suffer. These days, parents raise their children without giving them chores to do at home, and most children today don't have an opportunity to go to work with their parents, so they don't get that personal mentoring that I received. I was very fortunate.

If a person does not have a good work ethic before he meets Jesus Christ as Savior, then that is something he or she must change. Knowing Jesus should make us the very best workers in the workplace. We represent the Lord in this world, and God is our provider. In fact, *Jehovah Jireh,* a compound name for God in the Old Testament means, "The Lord is my provider."

If our job is where we represent God, then we should represent Him very well by doing the very best job we can with the very best attitude. We should have the best relationships with fellow employees and use the cleanest language. We should be the fastest learners, the most honest, the most punctual, the come-early-and-stay late employees in the place. If you owned a business, you would want employees like that, wouldn't you?

The Bible teaches that we should be ambitious people, not lazy. Proverbs contains many illustrations of Bible teaching on work ethics:

- Proverbs 6:6-8 says, "Go to the ant, O sluggard, observe her ways and be wise, which, having no chief, officer or ruler, prepares her food in the summer, and gathers her provision in the harvest." The writer of Proverbs addresses his readers as "sluggards" or lazy ones. He suggests they take a lesson from the ant, who works constantly, driven by an internal force rather than by a chief or officer or ruler. The ant gathers its food in the summer and gathers the winter's provision in the harvest. So should we do, driven by our relationship with Jesus, and not because the boss is watching. We should gather provisions (accumulate assets) for the time we know we will not be able to work.

- Proverbs 30:24 says, "Four things are small on the earth, but they are exceedingly wise." In Proverbs, being *wise* represents following God's will, often personified as the Lord Jesus Himself.
- Proverbs 30:25 says, "The ants are not a strong people, but they prepare their food in the summer." This verse introduces us to one of those little creatures that display wisdom (God's will) for us.
- Proverbs 30:26 says, "The shephanim [badgers] are not mighty people, yet they make their houses in the rocks."

Working hard and preparing for the future is God's will for us. Wisdom, God's will, is not just instructing us about the structural integrity of the house in which we live, but about the security and stability with which we live. Proverbs 30:27 says, "The locusts have no king, yet all of them go on in ranks." God put it in the locusts to work together as a team. So we should be the best team member, complimenting and motivating the people we work with.

Now go back to Proverbs 6:9-11 to see what God thinks of being lazy.

"How long will you lie down, O sluggard? When will you arise from your sleep? 'A little sleep, a little slumber, a little folding of the hands to rest'—Your poverty will come in like a vagabond, and your need like an armed man."

In the parable of the talents, Jesus let us know what He thinks of being lazy. The master in Jesus' parable said this to the servant who did nothing with the talent he had received: "You wicked, lazy slave, you knew that I reap where I did not sow and gather where I scattered no seed" (Matthew 25:26).

We should have enthusiasm for our work, and all of life, for that matter. The word *enthusiasm* is from two Greek words, *ice* meaning "in or into," and *theos,* the word for "God" or "in God." The definition of *enthusiasm* is a spirit of intense zeal, but that is what having God in our lives should do for us—it should give us a spirit of intense, but gentle, zeal.

Diligence is another word used in the Bible to describe our work. Proverbs 10:4 says, "Poor is he who works with a negligent hand, but the hand of the diligent makes rich."

According to *Webster's New World College Dictionary* the definition of *diligence* is, "the faithful applications to one's work."

Romans 12:11 says, "Not lagging behind in diligence, fervent in spirit, serving the Lord." The Bible teaches us in 1 Corinthians 10:31, "Whether, then, you eat or drink or whatever you do, do all to the glory of God."

How this mindset would change the world's view of Christian people if we would live like this!

If we can believe God's promises, we will have a whole new attitude toward our work. God has said this in Deuteronomy 28:10-12:

So all the peoples of the earth will see that you are called by the name of the LORD, and they will be afraid of you. The

LORD will make you abound in prosperity, in the offspring of your body and in the offspring of your beast and in the produce of your ground, in the land which the LORD swore to your fathers to give you. The LORD will open for you His good storehouse, the heavens, to give rain to your land in its season and to bless all the work of your hand; and you shall lend to many nations, but you shall not borrow."

God has promised to bless all that we do, so we need to learn to do all that He says. We should be comforted and encouraged to know God has promised to bless all that we put our hand to, to open heaven and pour out blessings, to make us abound in prosperity. It is important for us to know God has put it in us to make wealth.

Deuteronomy 8:18 says, "But you shall remember the LORD your God, for it is He who is giving you power to make wealth, that He may confirm His covenant which He swore to your fathers, as it is this day."

Our commitment is to work out of the salvation God has put in us, and adopting a good work ethic is a part of that. We can make up our minds to be ambitious and not lazy, enthusiastic and diligent, knowing in our hearts that we are blessed by God and we represent Him in this world. We become thoroughly convinced that God will bless all that we put our hand to, so we put our hand to as much as possible.

God has promised those who have been restored to Him in Jesus Christ that He would establish for them a renowned planting place. God gave this promise to Israel through the prophet Ezekiel:

"I will establish for them a renowned planting place, and they will not again be victims of famine in the land, and they will not endure the insults of the nations anymore."

—Ezekiel 34:29

Today's renowned planting place is wherever the Christian happens to be when he is restored to full fellowship with God. This is the one who has put on Jesus' attitude, works hard, does his best at everything he does, and manages the produce of his labor as God's Word and the Holy Spirit instructs him. Then you will experience the fulfillment of Jeremiah 29:11:

"For I know the plans that I have for you," declares the Lord, "plans for welfare and not calamity to give you a future and a hope."

CHAPTER 5

PLANNING

In all your ways acknowledge Him, and He shall direct your paths.

—Proverbs 3:6 NKJV

PLANNING IS THE process of identifying goals and converting them into activities that provide a step-by-step program that controls our thoughts and actions each day. If we are going to be where we want to be in six months, a year, five years, or twenty years, we need to know what to do today to make progress toward those goals. Planning is important to put action to our faith. Without planning, our goals are only dreams that will never be realized. Consider the weightlifter who sets a goal of lifting a certain weight. In order to reach that goal, he must plan a training routine, including workouts, diet, and rest. So, too, if we are to reach a financial goal, we need to plan a money management routine, including spending and saving. Planning is the action that follows commitment and good intentions. It is where we confront the frustration and either rise to faith and praise, or sink into despair and unbelief. Our planning sessions should begin with prayer and Bible study, as the Lord has directed us in Proverbs 3:6: "In all your ways acknowledge Him, and He shall direct your paths" (NKJV).

When a weight lifter plans a workout routine, he firmly believes he can reach the goal he has set for himself, even though that goal may require all his ability, energy, and discipline. We must believe we can reach the goal or we will not be motivated to put forth the energy and discipline to do each day what we plan.

Proverbs 16:9 says, "The mind of man plans his way, but the Lord directs his steps." We must always leave room for the Holy Spirit's leading. He may bless you with miracles, or test you by allowing obstacles to come up in your life that must be overcome. This only strengthens your faith and your resolve. It is not our plan that we really want, but God's. Our plans are our attempts to put what we know about God's will into action.

Proverbs 19:21 says, "Many are the plans in a man's heart, but the counsel of the LORD will stand." Don't forget the value of good counselors or advisers who really know what they are talking about. Proverbs 15:22 says, "Without consultation, plans are frustrated, but with many counselors they succeed." You should be ready to begin, armed with a ledger and note pad, your balance sheet, income and expense analysis, a calculator, your Bible, and a copy of your goals, both long-term and short-term. Sit down with the one who shares the decision-making process with you. Start with prayer, thanking God for His plans for you (your goals) and asking His help in your planning. Give Him permission to change your plans as you go.

Goal # 1: Plan to Get Out of Debt

One of your goals will be to get out of debt and stay out, so you need to start paying more on your debts. If they are credit cards, start paying extra on the ones with the highest interest. And, of course, stop using them if at all possible. If one of the debts is a mortgage or a vehicle, designate the extra payment to the principal so that it won't go to future interest. If you don't have extra money, you may have to find it by identifying frivolous spending and putting a stop to it. Please do not stop tithing to get extra money for debt reduction.

Here's another suggestion. Want to add hundreds a month to your available money? You may need to get better control of your meal planning. Plan your meals for a month in advance, and shop for groceries at discount stores, buying in quantity so you won't shop so often.

- Clipping coupons: this can be time consuming, but it can also be very fun and very rewarding. Just make sure you don't use having a discount coupon as an excuse to buy something you don't need or wouldn't otherwise buy.
- Stop smoking. Now I'm meddling, but smoking is one of the most expensive things you can do.
- Get rid of extra phone lines and all those services the phone company adds to your bill each month.
- Get rid of the cell phone if you don't absolutely need it.
- Change to a less expensive long distance telephone company and get control of your long distance calling.

- Raise the deductible on your car insurance to five hundred dollars. If it's paid for and not worth much, drop the collision and comprehensive. Never drop the liability.
- Cash in those whole life insurance policies and replace them with term life insurance in the amount your family needs if you die.
- Don't use premium gasoline—buy regular.
- Don't carry large sums of money. You are more prone to spend it. Carry only small amounts of cash.
- Stay out of stores and avoid those recreational shopping trips.
- If your hobby or form of recreation is expensive, change it to something less expensive, or better yet, one with no expense at all.
- If you can, carpool or ride a bus to work instead of driving your car and paying for parking.
- Drink water instead of all those sodas; you will be surprised how much this will save.
- If you rent, consider a less expensive place.
- If you have a mortgage and your interest rate is two percent above the current rate, consider refinancing to lower payments and/or shorten the mortgage. Only in extreme situations should you consider taking equity out of your house to pay bills.
- If your kids are addicted to ice cream and you can't wean them, put some in the freezer and don't let them fleece you of six or seven dollars every time they hear that stupid little bell.

- Set your thermostat up a couple degrees in summer and down a couple in winter. This helps a lot more than you may realize.
- Set your water heater temperature just a little lower.
- Rent home movies instead of going to movies.
- If you go to ball games, put yourself on a budget and don't spend a fortune on hot dogs, soft drinks, and such.
- Consider basic cable instead of all those movie channels.
- Take your lunch to work instead of eating out.
- Check into paying bills electronically. This saves postage and may save on late fees.
- Another possibility is to pay your bill six months to a year at a time on those bills that are fixed. Sometimes you get a discount or a free month for doing this.
- If you get a tax refund every year, consider filling out a new W-4 form at work so you get that money now instead of at tax time. The money will be there somewhere, you'll just have to find it.

A lot of these suggestions won't fit you, but it may get you thinking so you will find the ones that do fit you.

Goal # 2: Budget a Cash Reserve

Another goal will be to have and live out of a cash reserve. So you need to start a savings account and add to it from every paycheck; even if it is just five dollars, add something every month. Eventually, you will be putting hundreds or thousands each month into your cash reserve. Your goal needs to be at least six months' living expenses in your cash reserve. As it grows beyond your goal money, it can be swept off to better and more productive investments.

Your planning will produce a budget. Many people don't like that word, but a budget is only your written plan. Think of the weight lifter who writes down his training routine, diet, and sleep times needed to reach his target. Similarly, we need a written plan and we need to stick to it to the best of our abilities.

As your budget begins to unfold and develop, be willing to make adjustments until it is perfect for you. You will need to develop a debt management strategy, a risk management strategy, and an investment strategy. Acquiring the strategies may require some basic education.

You will need to begin your education at the same time you begin your budget. Visit the library and bookstores, and don't neglect the Christian book store. You want to learn as much as possible and as fast as possible. God will lead you by using the storehouse of your knowledge. Biblical examples are many, including Solomon, who asked God to give him wisdom when he became King of Israel (1 Kings 3:11-12).

Notice these truths from Proverbs:

- How blessed is the man who finds wisdom and the man who gains understanding. (3:13)
- Acquire wisdom! Acquire understanding. (4:5)
- Buy truth, and do not sell it, get wisdom and instruction and understanding. (23:23)

Keep the checkbook balanced accurately and create a fun way to keep track of how fast debts are paid down and savings are going up. Perhaps make a graph or chart of some kind and put it up somewhere to keep you reminded.

Finally, remember this exhortation the apostle Paul offers from God:

> "But we urge you ... to make it your ambition to lead a quiet life and attend to your own business and work with your hands, just as we commanded you, so that you may behave properly toward outsiders and not be in any need."
> —1 Thessalonians 4:10-12

CHAPTER 6

UNDERSTANDING DEBT

"The LORD will open for you His good storehouse, the heavens, to give rain to your land in its season and to bless all the work of your hand; and you shall lend to many nations, but you shall not borrow."

—Deuteronomy 28:12

THE BIBLE IS emphatic about several subjects that pertain to money. One of these subjects is what God has said about debt. If we wake up some morning and discover we are in debt, we need to get busy and do something about it with some urgency.

Once again, listen to God's Word from the book of Proverbs:

- A man lacking in sense pledges and becomes guarantor in the presence of his neighbor. (17:18)
- Do not be among those who give pledges, among those who become guarantors for debts. If you have nothing

with which to pay, why should he take your bed from under you? (22:26-27)

- He who is guarantor for a stranger will surely suffer for it, but he who hates being a guarantor is safe. (11:15)
- My son, if you have become surety for your neighbor,
  Have given a pledge for a stranger,
  If you have been snared with the words of your mouth,
  Have been caught with the words of your mouth,
  Do this then, my son, and deliver yourself;
  Since you have come into the hand of your neighbor,
  Go, humble yourself, and importune your neighbor.
  Give no sleep to your eyes,
  Nor slumber to your eyelids;
  Deliver yourself like a gazelle from the hunter's hand
  And like a bird from the hand of the fowler. (6:1-5)

Don't Get Caught up in the World's Ways

These verses cause us to think there is some urgency about getting out of debt. Indeed, Jesus suggests there is. He teaches us to pray in this way about debt: "... and forgive us our debts, as we forgive our debtors" Matthew 6:12 (KJV).

The word for debts in Matthew is the Greek word for financial debts—not surprising to see that Matthew was a tax collector. Ultimately, God's Word tells us that debt is a result of doing business with the world in the world's way. We must repent and change by first asking God's forgiveness, then by doing the things that will get us out of debt and keep us out. Debt happens because we turn our hearts from God's way to the world's way, or perhaps we have never learned God's way. In any case, wanting things, raising our standard of living beyond our means, and using debt are all the world's ways and Christians should not get caught in those traps. When we discover that we have, we must work hard to get out.

> "There is precious treasure and oil in the dwelling of the wise, but a foolish man swallows it up."
>
> —Proverbs 21:20

It may happen like this: A person goes shopping and sees something he or she wants. He did not know he wanted that thing until he saw it. That's what shopping does: It creates wants.

So the person bows his head to God and prays, "Lord, can I have it?" The still small voice replies, "Do you have the money? Does it fit in the plan?" The obvious answer is no. The person walks away disappointed.

Now comes the demon called "Consumption" with a plan. He whispers, "Look, God has promised to meet all your needs, hasn't He? If you put it on a credit card, you can add it to your bills, and all your bills are needs, aren't they?"

I know it's not that simple. We don't always hear God's voice so clearly, and we don't want to hear the enemy's voice at all. But in actuality, we end up putting the results of our impulse buying in our needs list that we present to God, reminding Him that He has promised to meet our needs. When He doesn't, we feel hurt, confused, and discouraged, and we wonder why His promises don't pertain to us. In this example, we have not only tried to manipulate God, but we have gone into debt. By doing so, we become obligated to a new master.

"The rich rules over the poor, and the borrower becomes the lender's slave" (Proverbs 22:7). When we owe someone money, that person becomes our master. If you doubt this, just get behind and you will realize you have even given up the right to be treated civilly. Collection departments and collection agencies can and do say very ugly things to people who owe them money.

Many people focus on the words that appear at the end of Deuteronomy 28:12—"But you shall not borrow"—and they ignore the words preceding them, "And you shall lend to many nations." God does not say never to use credit. He does tell us not to go into debt and don't be the borrower, but we can, and should, be the lender:

> "For the LORD your God will bless you as He has promised you, and you will lend to many nations, but you will not borrow …"
>
> —Deuteronomy 15:6

When you open a savings account, you lend your money to the bank. When you buy a treasury bill or a savings bond, you lend your money to the U.S. government. When you buy a corporate bond, you lend your money to that corporation. When you buy a utility bond or a municipal bond, you lend your money to that utility company or that municipality. You will certainly accumulate assets if you buy all these bonds, but we are not supposed to stop there.

Be a Gracious Lender

Psalm 112:5-6 says, "It is well with the man who is gracious and lends; He will maintain his cause in judgment. For he will never be shaken; the righteous will be remembered forever."

The Bible teaches emphatically that we are to be lenders, not only for the investment value of lending to many nations, but to individuals who come to us for help. It is one way God shows His love for people through us. Jesus confirms this teaching:

> "If you lend to those from whom you expect to receive, what credit is that to you? Even sinners lend to sinners, in order to receive back the same amount. But love your enemies, and do good, and lend, expecting nothing in return; and your reward will be great, and you will be sons of the Most High; for He Himself is kind to ungrateful and evil men. Be merciful, just as your Father is merciful."
>
> —Luke 6:34-36

God wants us to value people, even our enemies, above money, and to help them, lending to them with no expectation of getting it back. It is an expression of our love for Him. We should never turn away from someone who has come to us in need. To do so is to value our possessions above a soul for whom Jesus died.

People need our love a lot more than they need our money, but often money is an expression of love. We must be sensitive to the Holy Spirit's leading in this matter. You don't need to worry about losing money, for God has said if you give to the poor, you are lending to God, and He certainly can be trusted to repay you.

Take this promise as your own: "One who is gracious to a poor man lends to the LORD, and He will repay him for his good deed" (Proverbs 19:17). Jesus carries this wisdom further in His Sermon on the Mount as recorded in Matthew 5:42: "Give to him who asks of you, and do not turn away from him who wants to borrow from you." You should never turn away a brother or sister who comes to you for help.

Modern day worldly Christianity wants to judge why the need occurred before deciding whether or not to help. This is not to be done. You are not to be a judge, but an expression of God's love. The person may need help beyond a loan, or he or she may need something different than a money loan. But when you do lend him money, it is just that—a loan. God Himself will repay you, even if the borrower cannot or will not. When money comes from any source, it is from God. If it comes from an unexpected source, it may be that God is repaying you as He said He would. As for the borrower, let him know it is a loan, and let him repay it if he can, but in your heart, release him from that debt. After all, it is not your money, but God's money you are managing.

Never badger someone or go collecting on the debt. When the Holy Spirit nudges you, go to the borrower and release him from the debt. If God repays it to you, go to the borrower and tell him, "God has repaid it," and release him. Do not try to collect it twice, once from God and again from the borrower.

We must be careful how we treat those in need, because we can reproach God or honor Him simply by the way we react to that one who comes to us for help. Proverbs 14:31 assures us, "He who oppresses the poor taunts his Maker, but he who is gracious to the needy honors Him."

> "If there is a poor man with you, one of your brothers, in any of your towns in your land which the LORD your God is giving you, you shall not harden your heart, nor close your hand from your poor brother; but you shall freely open your hand to him, and shall generously lend him sufficient for his need in whatever he lacks. Beware that there is no base thought in your heart, saying, 'The seventh year, the year of remission,

is near,' and your eye is hostile toward your poor brother, and you give him nothing; then he may cry to the LORD against you, and it will be a sin in you. You shall generously give to him, and your heart shall not be grieved when you give to him, because for this thing the LORD your God will bless you in all your work and in all your undertakings. For the poor will never cease to be in the land; therefore I command you, saying, 'You shall freely open your hand to your brother, to your needy and poor in your land.'"

—Deuteronomy 15:7-11

Like the rest of the Law, these commandments are fulfilled in Jesus Christ. Only Jesus can put it in our hearts to care enough about managing money properly and yet be willing to help those around us who are in need without being concerned about whether we get paid back. We are not to judge how a person got into the need. We are only to be an expression of God's love in the person's life, and that means more than just saying, "Go your way, be warmed and filled, may your faith make you whole." James 2:15-16 describes that useless and loveless attitude:

"If a brother or sister is without clothing and in need of daily food, and one of you says to them, 'Go in peace, be warmed and be filled' and yet you do not give them what is necessary for their body, what use is that?"

The Bible says we are not to borrow, but also says we are not to judge or turn away those who want to borrow from us. The Bible tells us to be gracious and lend to those who want to borrow from us. At first, the teaching that we are not to borrow but we are not to prohibit those who want to borrow from us seems like a contradiction, does it not? But if you can, simply compare this situation about money with other life experiences that our relationship with the Lord Jesus changes. For instance, one Christian may have grown in Christ so that he does not watch any violence on television, but he should not ridicule or belittle those who have not come to that same conviction—you never know what is going on in a person's life. You might meet someone who really does not believe in borrowing. He might be like Job: God has put him in that situation to show the world His light or faith. God sometimes allows His people to go though difficult situations to demonstrate that financial problems do not have to damage your relationship with God. In this case, a person will not ask for a loan. But if you know about his situation, the question is, "Are you supposed to help?" If so, in what way? His situation becomes a test for you. Ask God and He will show you what you should do: you, not him.

I will share a personal testimony. Years ago, I went through a series of problems, culminating in bone cancer. After a three-year battle involving radiation, lots of chemotherapy, and a bone marrow transplant, I emerged from the ordeal very thankful to be alive. I was finally healthy, but very broke. This experience literally wiped out all our financial resources and severely limited my ability to earn a living. In desperation, I went to a close friend who was a millionaire. I humbly asked to borrow some money so I would not lose my house and car. To my surprise, he simply told me he did not have a very good track record in getting repaid in this kind of lending. He also told me to move into the city union mission (a ministry for the homeless) or to live out of my car. After all, he said, there were only the two of us, my wife and me.

His counsel is an object lesson of what not to do. The question 1 John 3:17 raises could not be more clear : "But whoever has the world's goods, and sees his brother in need and closes his heart against him, how does the love of God abide in him?"

It was a struggle to forgive this unchristian act, but we have.

CHAPTER 7

LIVE OUT OF CASH

> There is one who pretends to be rich, but has nothing; another pretends to be poor, but has great wealth.
>
> —Proverbs 13:7

THE VERSE ABOVE is a strange one. People often misunderstand it. So what is its message?

It simply describes the difference between one who lives out of cash and one who lives out of debt. This wise observation means that if you are not a spender, if you are not trying to keep up with the Joneses, and if you are not trying to impress anyone with your possessions, you will have great wealth.

Proverbs 21:20 says, "There is precious treasure and oil in the dwelling of the wise, but a foolish man swallows it up." *Never, never, never* use credit for anything consumable or that depreciates in value. It is so tempting to put things on credit. Using credit for groceries, movies, or gasoline is quick and easy, but extremely dangerous. The best thing to do when that credit card bill comes is to pay the whole thing. Most companies won't charge interest if the balance due is paid off within thirty days.

Build Up a Cash Reserve

But … the real temptation is to pay only the minimum payment, so we can spend our cash on something else. In time, we only have enough money to pay the minimum, because the balance has grown so we can't pay the whole thing. If you use a credit card for consumables, use it like cash and pay it off every month. Be determined never to pay one penny in interest for anything consumable, ever. *Living out of cash* means keeping things paid for. We should continually keep six months to one-year living expenses in cash reserve and live out of that reserve.

We should also pay cash for appliances like washers and dryers, refrigerators, even furniture, because they depreciate in value, and if we buy them on credit, often they wear out before we have finished paying for them. Not to mention the fact that if we add up the total of payments, we discover that we have paid double or even triple the price compared to paying cash.

Even our automobile should be paid for up front because autos depreciate in value. Try this alternative to taking out a loan: Keep the car you have three years beyond the last payment, only put into a bank the same amount as the payment. You will accumulate enough to pay for a new car. Then build into your cash reserve a planned purchase of the next new car when that one is used up.

Keep a Journal of Your Expenses

To manage your cash reserve like this takes planning, discipline, and knowledge. You must know how much you spend on everything—food, toilet articles, utilities, gas, cleaning, and/ or laundry, medical, virtually everything. Plan for those expenses and stick to your plan. You must predict vacations, Christmas spending, birthday gifts, appliance replacement, car maintenance and/ or repair, everything possible, and plan for them by putting aside enough money in cash reserve to pay for them when they occur.

We should keep six months' to one-year's worth of living expenses in cash reserve and live out of that reserve. We must be disciplined enough to stop our impulse buys, both large and small. It also takes discipline to stay on top of the information, balancing the checkbook, adjusting the plan, and determining the amount needed.

Keep a journal of all the things you need cash for beyond the normal living expenses. They may be things like purchasing snow tires before winter, having the chimney cleaned, money for Christmas gifts, sending the kids to summer camp, and taking vacations. If you have trouble keeping funds designated, open several savings accounts. I like to use a mutual fund money market account and then keep a journal to designate—you might try that. By journaling expenses, you won't be tempted to spend your reserve as it grows larger and larger; you will know that it is for a lot of little things you already have planned. If you do have extra money beyond all the things you plan for, invest it in a good growth mutual fund or stocks in some good solid companies.

Resist the temptation to raise your standard of living just because you have some extra money. Remember your long-term goals such as retirement, buying your own business, college for the kids (or yourself), supporting aging parents, and others in the future. Don't sacrifice those worthy goals just to raise your standard of living now.

Managing cash properly is the cutting edge of your plan. If you don't do it properly, the rest of your plan will not fall into place. But if you succeed in managing cash, the rest of your plan will automatically happen. At this point, we face all the temptation and frustration, because it takes time and discipline to stay on top of it. It is so easy to let it slide and get behind. Then it gets out of control, and we don't know where we are or how much we have.

CHAPTER 8

STANDARD OF LIVING

Do not love the world nor the things in the world.

—1 John 2:15

OUR STANDARD OF living is the amount of worldly goods (stuff) we expect to have, want to have, or think we deserve to have. It will be a result of our self-appraisal as well as our comparing of ourselves with other people. We formulate a self-image based on our background, our education, our job, our peer group, and probably many other factors. We see ourselves living in a certain kind of house, driving a certain kind of car, dressing a certain way.

Most people admit to living below the standard of living they desire, so most people strive to raise their standard of living. In this condition, the temptations the apostle Paul describes in 1 Timothy 6:9 become a reality:

"But those who want to get rich fall into temptation and a snare and many foolish and harmful desires which plunge men into ruin and destruction."

For most of us, our standard of living has not been planned; it is the result of our income and impulse buying, and has just evolved from the struggle between our dreams and reality. However it happens, raising our standard of living beyond God's will is to exalt ourselves, and Jesus warns against that desire:

"Whoever exalts himself shall be humbled; and whoever humbles himself shall be exalted."
—Matthew 23:12

In fact, God has commanded us to be humble:

"All of you, clothe yourselves with humility toward one another, for God is opposed to the proud, but gives grace to the humble. Humble yourselves, therefore, under the mighty hand of God, that He may exalt you at the proper time."
—1 Peter 5:5-6

God has promised us that if we refuse to humble ourselves, He will humble us. He has also promised to bless those who humble themselves. Being humble means a lot of things and touches all of life. It is an attitude that you can see. Being content with what we have, or even being willing to live with less stuff, is what being humble means financially. The less of our income our standard of living consumes, the more there is for investing and giving.

Usually, once we get concerned about our lack of giving or investing and the amount of our debt compared to our assets, we find ourselves having to lower our standard of living out of necessity. Lowering our standard of living out of necessity is always a very painful process. Sometimes we feel locked into our standard of living because we have financed everything, and those agreements are hard to get out of.

God wants us to reestablish our focus. First John 2:15-16 states what our attitude should be:

> "Do not love the world, nor the things in the world. If anyone loves the world, the love of the Father is not in him. For all that is in the world, the lust of the flesh and the lust of the eyes and the boastful pride of life, is not from the Father, but is from the world."

Some of the principles He wants us to live by reiterate what we have discussed in previous chapters, but they are so important that I am repeating them:

- Our standard of living should be a humble portion of our income.
- We should be out of debt and only use debt very wisely.
- We should invest and give out of every income check.
- We should live out of a cash reserve sufficient to handle living expenses for six months with no income.
- We should invest (accumulate) for identified future needs.
- We should be smart business people and run our personal finances as such.

God is certainly not opposed to us having things. He blessed the saints in the Bible with great wealth. Proverbs 10:22 states,

"It is the blessing of the LORD that makes rich, and He adds no sorrow to it." God does not want us to love this world or the things in it, but to love Him. He has created us and our eternal spirits to be capable of fellowship with Him and He has placed us in a mortal body. We must learn to walk in the Spirit completely, while living in the flesh. This is a paradox as mysterious as the incarnation of Jesus, who was God in the flesh. We must hold earthly things loosely, willing to turn loose quickly, not having our life revolve around things, but being totally committed to Him and our relationship with Him.

We are ambassadors for Him in this world: "Therefore, we are ambassadors for Christ" (2 Corinthians 5:20). As ambassadors, we know this world is not our home. We are citizens of heaven. God provides the things of this world to equip us to be ambassadors. If we can set our sights on the proper ways to manage our assets and on making our primary goal to be all He wants us to be, we will not fall into the traps of the world. We will be not only successful in the Spirit, but successful in the world, because He has shown us how and leads us personally by His Spirit.

Therefore, we need to turn loose our preconceived idea of what standard of living we deserve and be content with whatever God's will is for us. If God says, "Sell everything and follow Me," do it. If He says to downsize for reasons only He knows, do it. If He exalts you, accept the praise with thanksgiving, but don't fall in love with it.

Always be willing to go not only from the bottom to the top, but from the top to the bottom. Our hearts deceive us. We look at all the things we have and say to ourselves, "I could give all this up; it means nothing to me." We may really mean it, but our hearts deceive us; God knows our hearts, and sometimes He chooses to show us. We may be surprised with how tough it is to give up certain things, let alone everything.

I have just experienced that very thing, having had a three-year battle with cancer. I have the wonderful opportunity to start over at fifty-five years old. Trying to maintain our previous lifestyle, along with some very foolish mistakes, has been as hard as cancer was. For us to give up our feelings of entitlement to our previous standard of living, and instead to adopt an attitude like young newlyweds who start out only with their love for each other, can and should be a wonderful experience. As we sometimes do when we play Monopoly, we may just need to start the game over.

Perhaps that is the case with you. It's never too late and the devil is lying when he says it is. A good portion of today's millionaires got their start late in life. Many of them have started over several times. What they possessed was a willingness to learn from their mistakes and an attitude never to quit. We Christians, armed with God's promises and His presence, should do no less. In this respect, it is true that sometimes the children of the world are wiser than the children of God.

Now for some practical tips that I hope will help to keep that old standard of living under control.

- Don't be a spender. Learn to be the kind of person who can put a dollar in your pocket in the morning and still have it that night.
- Learn to fix things instead of buying new ones.
- Keep things paid for.
- Owe no one anything, ever.

- Strive to keep expenses low. It may take a constant vigilance to keep lights off that are not being used, and heat or air turned down or off when you are not home, but it is worth it.
- Learn to keep a storage pantry and live out of it, shopping only to restock it. Buy in quantity at discount stores.
- Plan meals and expenses well in advance.
- Live on a well-planned, up-to-date budget that is the result of prayer, planning, and counseling.

Don't let the enemy of our souls put you on a guilt trip. God is preparing a place for us far better than anything on earth, and absolutely nothing is too good for His bride. It's not that He doesn't want us to have the very best, but He is working on a different project than we are. God is working on that inner self, to change us into the image of Jesus Christ, so we will be ready for Him in that bridal chamber called heaven. And don't let "Ole Slewfoot" make you ashamed of your standard of living—our Lord Jesus lived humbly with no place of His own. It is hard to imagine anybody could live on a lower standard than Jesus, but we don't know that He ever wanted for anything, and so, too, all our needs will be met.

CHAPTER 9

INVESTING

A good man leaveth an inheritance to his children's children.
—Proverbs 13:22 KJV

INVESTING IS THE part of our money management that looks to the future. Many people never invest at all beyond buying a home and experiencing some appreciation in value over the years. The pressure from the world to raise our standard of living keeps most people from ever having any money to invest.

The Christian community has not helped Christians understand that they should invest. Misunderstanding about the laying up of treasures here on earth, and overzealous preaching about giving and tithing has left many Christians with the impression that they shouldn't invest. God's Word is very clear that we are responsible to provide for ourselves and our household: These words from 1 Timothy 5:8 are strong ones: "But if anyone does not provide for his own, and especially for those of his household, he has denied the faith and is worse than an unbeliever." Paul states this comment in the negative, but it has positive instructions for us.

We Must Accept Our Responsibility to Provide

We are to accept the responsibility of being the provider for our own. The term "his own" in this verse seems to refer to a larger group than just one's household. We are to leave an inheritance for two generations. Proverbs 13:22 says, "A good man leaveth an inheritance to his children's children" (KJV).

God promises to give us a future in Jeremiah 29:11, one of my favorite verses:

> "'For I know the plans that I have for you,' declares the Lord, 'plans for welfare and not calamity to give you a future and a hope.'"

In order to make this promise a reality in your life, we must follow God's direction. Proverbs 3:5-6 KJV says, "Trust in the LORD with all thine heart and lean not unto thine own understanding. In all thy ways acknowledge Him, and He shall direct thy paths."

His direction leads us to good things and His direction leads us to avoid calamities. This promise, along with other verses from all over God's Word, tells us to prepare for all the coming events in our lives that we can see, and to prepare as well as possible for those inevitable experiences that we can't see, both good and bad. We can see old age and retirement, college for the kids, and many other future events that God has put in our lives and hearts. The events that we can't see may be sickness, loss of home and possessions by storm or accident, or the loss or change of our job or career. We should be thoroughly convinced that this is what we should do, and do it with conviction. That having been established, we should be ready for some practical advice.

Take Some Practical Steps

- Start your investing by putting as much as possible into a cash reserve *first*. At first, a savings account will do. Eventually, you should deposit your income into this account, then transfer enough into your checking to meet expenses, pay bills, and provide cash for things such as gas and daily needs. By doing it this way, you are more apt to plan your expenses and keep them under control. If you deposit into your checking first, then move what is left to cash reserve, you may be tempted to let expenses go unchecked.

- When the balance in cash reserve reaches more than one thousand dollars, move your cash reserve to a good mutual fund money market with check writing privileges. Make sure you know what those check writing policies are and that they fit your needs. Most mutual fund money markets will let you write as many checks as you want, as long as they are more than five hundred dollars each, so a once-a-month transfer into your checking account will work fine. Be sure to check with your bank to see if it treats your money market check as a draft or a check. A check is credited immediately and a draft takes fifteen days. Now some banks have gone totally electronic and it takes less time. The interest you get from the mutual fund money market is an important consideration, but not perhaps the most important.

Services provided are perhaps most important—these
include convenience, safety, and availability.

- As your account grows, consider moving part of it into
a government securities fund to receive higher interest,
but make sure you can change from the money market
to the government fund with a phone call and without
sales charges. At this point, you are becoming a lender
to many nations—remember Deuteronomy 28:12? Set
a goal of six months' living in a liquid position. As your
goal is realized, it should become a limit. Money beyond
this should be aimed at those future needs.

Understand the Kinds of Investments

There are two kinds of investments: *loanership* and *ownership*.
There are three kinds of returns on those investments: interest,
dividends, and capital gains.

Loanership is a document stating that you have loaned your
money to someone in return for an interest paid to you. This
includes interest bearing checking, savings accounts, and bonds
of all kinds. United States government bonds are called *treasuries*.
A treasury bill is one year to maturity. A treasury note is two
to ten years to maturity. A treasury bond is ten to thirty years
to maturity. The longer the maturity, the higher the interest.
Cities, states, and counties borrow money and these are called
municipal bonds, normally federal tax free and state tax free in
the state of origin. Corporations borrow money and these are
called *corporate bonds.* All of these bonds are traded publicly
so they have liquidity, but they will fluctuate up and down in
value. If held until maturity they will pay the face amount of the
bond. To help the public determine the level of risk, there are

two bond-rating organizations, Moody and Standard & Poor's rating services. You may also want to hold these bonds in the form of mutual funds.

Ownership is a document that states you own or share ownership of something. Ownership positions provide the other two forms of return. *Dividends* are your share of the profits a company earns. *Capital gains* are the profits you make when you sell the company, your house, stocks, or anything else that you own. As you can well imagine, it is more risky to own something than to lend, so you need to learn how to calculate the risk. In Jesus' parable of the talents, Matthew 25:14-30, the master rewarded the two servants that had doubled His money, but what most people don't realize is that both servants subjected the master's money to considerable risk. One went to the market and traded, with it receiving a double return. The other went to the traders to do the same thing and received a double return. The one that took no risk Jesus condemned. The greater return you want or need, the greater the risk factor. Risk in the investment world is not like the chances of winning or losing in gambling; it is the amount of volatility or value fluctuation the investment experiences.

You should target your goals. Calculate the amount needed and how long before it is needed. Equipped with this information, along with the amount available for that goal, you can calculate the return needed. Now find the investments that provide that possible return and decide if you can tolerate the risk. Sweep off the excess from your cash reserves into stocks or stock mutual funds targeted at your goals.

You may also want to put money toward the development of your personal talents. God has said in Deuteronomy 8:18 that

He has put it in you to make wealth, so you have something in you that you need to develop. We each must find out what that is, whether music, art, mechanics, building something, rentals, landscaping, virtually anything.

Some folks have retirement plans at their job. Be sure to take part; participate as much as possible, especially get all the matching funds from your company if available. Remember, this is only a part of your retirement planning—there are also IRAs, both regular IRAs and Roth IRAs. Learn about these and use them as much as possible. I always recommend self-directed IRAs because you can invest them in virtually any investment vehicle in the marketplace. You should retain as much control of your money as possible. There are all kinds of experts who will take that control from you if you let them, but you are the one responsible to God, so you should keep the decision-making power for yourself. Learn what you are doing and do it with diligence.

Once you have made the decision to invest and have put into operation a plan that will make it possible, you will have also taken on the responsibility to do it properly. It is essential to make sure your education in financial matters includes learning about investments of all kinds. It is an exciting experience to be all you can be in Christ.

CHAPTER 10

GIVING

"Remember the words of the Lord Jesus, that He Himself
said, 'It is more blessed to give than to receive.'"

—Acts 20:35

THE APOSTLE PAUL'S charge to the Christians at Ephesus
reminds them, and us, of the teaching of Jesus. Blessings will
abound when you give. I love the sheer joy that comes from giving,
and I'm always a little uncomfortable to be the receiver of the
giving of someone else. I have been on both sides and I like to be
the giver far better. Jesus simply said to do it:

> "Give, and it will be given to you. They will pour into your
> lap a good measure—pressed down, shaken together, *and*
> running over. For by your standard of measure it will be
> measured to you in return."
>
> —Luke 6:38

What Jesus has said in this verse is amazing. What may be even more so is what He did not say. Jesus said to give and it would be given to you. So if we are givers, we must also learn to be receivers. Jesus said to give, and it would be given to us. It logically follows that Jesus' words have significance far beyond money—you give, and the principle is that you are going to get back what you have given. You give love, you are going to get back love. You give mercy, you are going to get back mercy. You give strength, you are going to get back strength. You give encouragement, you are going to get back encouragement. You give money, you are going to get back money. "Give and it will be given to you" is the positive side of another and equally important truth: "Do not be deceived, God is not mocked; for whatever a man sows, this he will also reap" (Galatians 6:7).

Your Giving Will Come Back to You in Blessings

Jesus does not say how much to give, but He does say how much will be given back to you. He says, "a good measure—pressed down, shaken together, and running over." All the translations put these words together to give us the impression that it is more than we can handle. In Jesus' day, the men wore robes and they would pick up the ends to make a sort of basket. The verse says the blessings "will pour into your lap;" the picture is of a man holding the corners of his robe and people pouring into that makeshift container so much that he can hardly lug the contents home. Jesus says the amount coming back to you will be in proportion to how much you have given—"by your standard of measure it will be measured to you in return." It is assumed that you are the one who decides how big your blessings are going to be when you decide how much to give.

Honor the Lord Through Your Giving

Jesus said to give; Proverbs says our giving honors the Lord. There are other ways to honor the Lord with our wealth, such as recognizing His ownership, living humbly, not getting into debt, not being a spender, and the like, but giving is an essential way of honoring Him. It gives God glory and produces praise for Him.

Proverbs 3:9-10 is God's promise to bless you when you honor the Lord with your wealth. There are many passages in God's Word that instruct us to give, and without fail, each one has its corresponding promise to bless you if you do. God searches our hearts and there is a very real challenge to our motives—we are not to give to get, or give out of greed, but it is proper to get to give.

Proverbs 11:24-25 says, "There is one who scatters, and yet increases all the more, and there is one who withholds what is justly due, and yet it results only in want. The generous man will be prosperous, and he who waters will himself be watered."

In this image, the giver is a sower who walks along, slinging seeds right and left. That would imply giving in lots of places, wouldn't it? Notice how this verse says that each place we give is justly due and not to give is to withhold what is justly due: "There is one who withholds what is justly due, but it results only in want" (Proverbs 11:24). Not to give as the Lord directs us brings us to poverty and want instead of blessings.

Proverbs 3:6 affirms, "In all thy ways acknowledge Him, and He shall direct thy paths" (KJV). It is the Holy Spirit who should make the decisions about where and what to give. God is a giver, and He wants us to be givers. When Jesus gave instructions to the twelve apostles He sent out ahead of Him, He stated, "Freely you received, freely give" (Matthew 10:8). If God is the owner of all we have and He is a giver, then every dollar we have and every possession we have, no matter what it is, is subject to us giving it away under the leadership of the Holy Spirit.

When God nudges our heart to give something to someone, He is actually expressing His love for them. If we say no and don't do as He directs, we are withholding what is justly due and refusing to do the bidding of the Owner of the resources. I've stated this earlier, but it's so important that I will repeat it: Think of yourself as a trustee. God is the *grantor;* the *beneficiary* of the resources is whoever the grantor desires. The more precisely we follow His instruction, the more of His resources He can trust us with.

Giving provides the giver with a powerful influence in the lives of people. Proverbs 11:25 offers this promise: "The generous man will be prosperous, and he who waters will himself be watered." If you are a generous person and under the blessing of God, many people will be trying to win your favor. You will have many friends.

Proverbs 19:6-7 observes, "Many will seek the favor of a generous man, and every man is a friend to him who gives gifts. All the brothers of a poor man hate him; How much more do his friends abandon him! He pursues them with words, but they are gone."

The giver really does get blessed much more then the receiver does. The receiver is blessed by the size of the gift, but the giver is blessed many times that amount and in many different ways.

God Has Provided Us with Principles for Giving

Two full chapters from Paul's epistles to the Corinthian church, 2 Corinthians 8 and 9, provide for us with some solid principles on giving the way God wants His people to experience it:

- "Now, brethren, we wish to make known to you the grace of God which has been given in the churches of Macedonia" (2 Corinthians 8:1). Paul points out this is a grace, not a law. If you give out of grace, you follow the Holy Spirit speaking to you in your heart. If you give out of bondage to the law or because you merely obey what the law commands you to do, you will not receive the blessings and you will not be under the instruction of the Holy Spirit. You are not going to be free. You are going to be bound up in legalism. You will find yourself giving grudgingly. Giving is the expression of God's love to you and through you.

- "That in a great ordeal of affliction and their abundance of joy and their deep poverty overflowed in the wealth of their liberality" (8:2). Their giving was out of a great ordeal of affliction. They had abundance of joy, and it came out of deep poverty. It was the first time these Christians had experienced giving. They had learned something new from the Holy Spirit and it was this grace called giving. They had learned not only how the Holy Spirit could lead them, but how the Holy Spirit could bless them, and how they could be in a channel of God's provision. God wants us to be like Jesus. In fact, that is what He is doing in our life—every experience in life is the Holy Spirit's opportunity to teach us and make us more like Jesus. We are supposed to love as He loves. We are supposed to feel what He feels. We are supposed to have His mind and think what He thinks. In every way, we are supposed to become more like Jesus all the time. Jesus is a provider, in fact, He is *the Provider,* and He wants us to have the opportunity to know what it is like to be a provider. It feels good to be a provider.

- "For you know the grace of our Lord Jesus Christ, that though He was rich, yet for your sake He became poor, so that you through His poverty might be rich" (8:9). Believe everything this verse says. We believe that He became sin so that we could be forgiven for sin. We believe that He died so we could live and we receive that by faith. Just like we receive health and healing, we receive wealth and prosperity. We just receive it because it is ours from Jesus.

- "For if the readiness is present, it is acceptable according to what a person has, not according to what he does not have" (8:12). If the Holy Spirit has touched your heart and taught you truth about giving, you are ready to begin managing God's money under His leadership. Simply bow your head and tell Him so.

- "Now this I say, he who sows sparingly will also reap sparingly; and he who sows bountifully will also reap bountifully" (9:6). Here is the same principle Jesus states in Luke 6:38: As you measure, it will be measured to you again.

- "Each one must do just as he has purposed in his heart, not grudgingly or under compulsion, for God loves a cheerful giver" (9:7). A paraphrase of the first part of this passage might be "Let each one do as he hears from God in his heart." It is not your heart that makes the decision. It is God who makes the decision and the

Holy Spirit communicates that to your heart. He tells us in our hearts what He wants us to do. Let each one give as he or she hears God in his heart. We make one decision—that is to do what God says to do. Then we have the responsibility to hear what He says. We have a little peek into the heart of God in His words "for God loves a cheerful giver."

The word "cheerful" in Greek is *hilaros.* Our word "hilarious" comes from that word. It almost means the same as our understanding of "hilarious." We might say someone is "laughing hilariously," and mean he or she is out of control. That person may be rolling on the ground, his sides hurting, and grinning until his face has cramped up. God means just that when it comes to giving. God loves a hilarious giver.

There are two ways you can be hilarious, out of control, in your giving. It could make you so happy that you are absolutely hilarious, or the amount of your giving could be in such a proportion that it is hilarious. The widow who gave her two mites gave hilariously in Mark 12:42 because she gave all she had. Abraham gave hilariously when He offered Isaac on the altar of sacrifice. God Himself gave hilariously when He offered His only Son on the cross for our sins.

My dad has given me an example of hilarious giving that is really close to my heart. Shortly after we—my parents, siblings, and myself—all accepted Christ in a church we visited in Colorado Springs, my dad and mom decided God wanted them to put their life savings into their church's building fund. Daddy had purchased eighty acres of land and he intended for that to provide his retirement. He sold the property and put it all in the church for a new building. When we kids found out about it, we hit the ceiling. "You can't give away your life savings! What is going to happen? We are going to end up supporting you the rest of your life!"

It was hilarious for a man who worked for the county, who was the father of five kids, and who made as little as he did to give that kind of gift. Daddy said, "Jerry, it belongs to God. It's His land. It's His money. I'm His, and He said 'give it.' He is going to take care of us, and besides that, the Lord is coming before I get old, anyway." That is hilarious giving. The wonder of it is that God did take care of him gloriously until his death at age eighty-one.

What can you do with this example? You can roll on the ground and laugh. You can say he was either crazy or he had a line to heaven. Looking back on his life, I am confident the truth is crystal clear: he had a line to heaven.

- "And God is able to make all grace abound to you, so that always, having all sufficiency in everything, you may have an abundance for every good deed" (9:8). God loves a cheerful giver and God is able to make all grace abound to you. If you believe this, you will no longer believe that your salary is the source of your income. You will believe that God is your provider and He is the source of your income. He is not limited by your job or your salary. He is not limited at all.

God knows our hearts. Years ago, when we were in financial and spiritual bondage, I tempted God in a very sinful way. I did not have enough money to pay my bills, so I looked up those verses that said God would give back more in return. I gave our money to the church and held up the verses to God and said "OK, I gave. Now you provide enough to pay the bills." I was trying to force God to bless me. It's a wonder He didn't kill me on the spot. You can't give out of greed and expect God to bless. I can imagine Him now, sitting on His throne, shaking His head in wonder, and saying, "When is that boy going to grow up?" The truth is, the boy is still growing up.

Second Corinthians 9:9-15 offers a picture of a giving church whose liberality produces praise and thanksgiving to God:

> "As it is written, 'He scattered abroad, He gave to the poor, His righteousness endures forever.' Now He who supplies seed to the sower and bread for food will supply and multiply your seed for sowing and increase the harvest of your righteousness; you will be enriched in everything for all liberality, which through us is producing thanksgiving to God. For the ministry of this service is not only fully supplying the needs of the saints, but is also overflowing through many thanksgivings to God. Because of the proof given by this ministry, they will glorify God for your obedience to your confession of the gospel of Christ and for the liberality of your contribution to them and to all, while they also, by prayer on your behalf, yearn for you because of the surpassing grace of God in you. Thanks be to God for His indescribable gift!"

Most of the members of the Corinthian church to whom the apostle Paul wrote were Gentile believers. They were taking up an offering for Jewish believers in Jerusalem. The Jewish believers were slow to accept the Gentiles as brothers. There were sects of Jewish believers that persecuted the Gentile believers and would not even permit them to come into their fellowship. In fact, when they first started winning Gentile believers, Peter was so influenced by them that Paul confronted him to his face. When the Jewish believers fell into great need due to persecution, the Gentile believers had a chance to demonstrate the love of God by collecting an offering for them. They showed their love by giving to the ones who hated them. It's been my experience when someone receives a gift from a giver, they turn immediately from the giver and look straight into heaven and say, "Thank you, God."

The things Jesus did not say in Luke 6:38 are not without answers in the Word of God. It is as if He wants us to look to Him and the Holy Spirit as each opportunity for giving arises. To be a giver is to "have this attitude in yourselves which was also in Christ Jesus" (Philippians 2:5), and to decide when, where, and how much is to come from the leadership of the Holy Spirit in our hearts.

God Has Provided Commandments About Giving

The word *tithe* as it appears in the Bible is the place to start. God gave Moses His commandments about the proper amount and place to give. Leviticus 27:30-33 records the words God told Moses to pass on to the people of Israel:

> "Thus all the tithe of the land, of the seed of the land or of the fruit of the tree, is the LORD's; it is holy to the LORD. If,

therefore, a man wishes to redeem part of his tithe, he shall add to it one-fifth of it. And for every tenth part of herd or flock, whatever passes under the rod, the tenth one shall be holy to the LORD. He is not to be concerned whether it is good or bad, nor shall he exchange it; or if he does exchange it, then both it and its substitute shall become holy. It shall not be redeemed."

The situation was different for Israel than it is for us, but we can still draw valuable instructions from it. Israel was divided into twelve tribes, one of which was the tribe of Levi. God gave this tribe the spiritual responsibilities for all Israel. They were to keep the temple, lead in all the worship, administer all the teaching; in short, they were to represent God among all the rest of the people. The holy land was divided among the other eleven tribes, but the tribe of Levi was not to own land; they were to live from the tithe of the other eleven tribes. A quick calculation reveals that when this was done properly, Levi would have a tenth more than the other tribes. This extra tenth was to be given to the priest for the service of the temple of God:

"Then the LORD spoke to Moses, saying, 'Moreover, you shall speak to the Levites and say to them, "When you take from the sons of Israel the tithe which I have given you from them for your inheritance, then you shall present an offering from it to the LORD, a tithe of the tithe."'"
—Numbers 18:25-26

It is easy to understand that when giving worked the way God intended, all Israel had equal shares of the Promised Land.

Tithe is a word that simply means "one tenth." They were to bring the tithe to the temple in Jerusalem.

> "But you shall seek the LORD at the place which the LORD your God will choose from all your tribes, to establish His name there for His dwelling, and there you shall come. There you shall bring your burnt offerings, your sacrifices, your tithes, the contribution of your hand, your votive offerings, your freewill offerings, and the firstborn of your herd and of your flock. There also you and your households shall eat before the LORD your God, and rejoice in all your undertakings in which the LORD your God has blessed you."
>
> —Deuteronomy 12:5-7

These verses make the beginning of our giving easy. The first tenth goes to the church where we are active and finding spiritual food. Many have taught that because Leviticus 27:30 teaches that the tithe is holy unto the Lord, the ninety percent left to you is not holy. This is totally wrong. You are holy because you belong to Jesus, and all that you have is holy, as well. The ninety percent left to you is as holy as is the tithe that you give to Him. The tithe is simply the place to start our giving, but it is by no means all there is to giving. Notice in Deuteronomy 12:6, how many other forms of offerings were to be brought to God with the tithe.

There Are Additional Ways to Give

The purpose of the tithe itself is to support our church. The next places of giving that comes to my mind are parachurch ministries. Much of the work of evangelizing the world, feeding the poor, and teaching and encouraging the saints is being done by ministries not connected directly to any church. I think of the Billy Graham Association, Samaritan's Purse, the Trinity Broadcasting network, and many others. I hesitate to name more for fear of naming ones you don't like or leaving one out. There are thousands of ministries, many of which are God-called and are doing an excellent job. These deserve your consideration, as well, especially if they are speaking into your life or if they are doing a work you care deeply about.

In addition to the list of offerings in Deuteronomy 12:6, there are many other forms of giving in the Old Testament, such as alms for the poor and support for widows and orphans. God also commanded the cancellation of debts in the year of Jubilee, and He commanded farmers to leave their outside rows unharvested so needy people could glean what was left behind. Hospitality was yet another form of giving: God's people were supposed to be hospitable to anyone traveling through who might be in need. They were supposed to help their neighbor if he was in trouble in any way.

Giving is all through the Bible, and it is not just through tithes and offerings. In the New Testament, we find this same principle stated in 1 John 3:17: "But whoever has the world's goods, and sees his brother in need and closes his heart against him, how does the love of God abide in him?"

If we interpret the word *brother* as someone in Christ Jesus, then we are to give to the saints whenever we see them in need.

John the Baptist, Jesus' cousin and forerunner, preached to the crowds by the Jordan River who questioned him about how to bear good fruit with words that still hold true today: "Let the man who has two tunics, share with him who has none and let him who has food do likewise" (Luke 3:11).

In addition to giving to other believers, God also directs us to give to people in our families:

> "But if anyone does not provide for his own, and especially for those of his household, he has denied the faith and is worse than an unbeliever."
>
> —1 Timothy 5:8

At least a part of keeping the faith is being a provider for our families. In Bible days, the households were the widest possible family unit, including fathers and mothers, children and grandchildren, uncles, aunts, and cousins. We must each prayerfully consider just who we are responsible for.

The poor must also be one of our opportunities to give. Jesus told the rich young ruler to sell all he had and give it to the poor (Luke 18:22). Proverbs 19:17 also says, "One who is gracious to a poor man lends to the LORD." If you are going to lend money to somebody, would you trust God? Would you give God a signature loan? I certainly would. If you give to the poor, it is like lending to God.

Consider these wise words about giving to the poor:

- "He who is generous will be blessed, for he gives some of his food to the poor" (Proverbs 22:9).
- "He who gives to the poor will never want, but he who shuts his eyes will have many curses" (Proverbs 28:27).
- "If there is a poor man with you, one of your brothers, in any of your towns in your land which the LORD your God is giving you, you shall not harden your heart, nor close your hand from your poor brother; but you shall

freely open your hand to him, and shall generously lend him sufficient for his need in whatever he lacks. Beware that there is no base thought in your heart, saying, 'The seventh year, the year of remission, is near,' and your eye is hostile toward your poor brother, and you give him nothing; then he may cry to the LORD against you, and it will be a sin in you. You shall generously give to him, and your heart shall not be grieved when you give to him, because for this thing the LORD your God will bless you in all your work and in all your undertakings" (Deuteronomy 15:7-10).

Where do you give? Give to the church, parachurch ministries, your family, the saints, the poor, even strangers. All are candidates for your liberality as the Lord directs your heart.

How much do you give? The answer to this question is not as easy, because it must be the personal instruction each of us gets from the Holy Spirit. We simply know that every dollar we have is subject to be given. If we understand that all that we have is God's, then we must understand that every dime, every dollar, is subject to be given as He directs. Normally, He doesn't direct us to give it all because He wants to take care of you. He wants us to take care of our family. He wants us to save and invest. He has all kinds of places for it. God looks at you and your welfare as a ministry because you are His. You are His bride. You are as important to Him as the church or anybody in the church, or any ministry that He has. You are His. So when God is providing for you, you are His ministry, and He also wants you to participate in ministry.

God wants to take care of you. Receive from Him. Let Him bless you. Let Him give you good things. Let Him exalt you, but do not exalt yourself. Be humble.

> "'For I know the plans that I have for you,' declares the LORD, 'plans for welfare and not for calamity to give you a future and a hope. Then you will call upon Me and come and pray to Me, and I will listen to you. And you will seek Me and find Me when you search for Me with all your heart. I will be found by you,' declares the LORD, 'and I will restore your fortunes.'"
>
> —Jeremiah 29:11-14a

CHAPTER 11

BONDAGE VS. FREEDOM

"If therefore the Son shall make you free, you shall be free indeed."

—John 8:36

SPIRITUAL BONDAGE PRODUCES financial bondage. Likewise, spiritual freedom produces financial freedom. We need to be free. Whether to choose financial bondage or financial freedom is a spiritual matter.

First, let's deal with financial bondage. This lesson came from my personal experience. It is my testimony and I am thankful to the Lord Jesus Christ for dealing with me.

Melinda and I were having terrible financial problems. It was killing us. We couldn't sleep; we couldn't do anything without the pressure of finances weighing us down. It seemed like every time I would get my hands on some money, some big disaster would come along and just blow it away. We wrestled with this for several years. Then one day I simply asked God, "Why?" He very gently told me to read Haggai, chapter 1:

> "'Is it time for you yourselves to dwell in your paneled houses while this house lies desolate?' Now therefore, thus says the LORD of hosts, 'Consider your ways! You have sown much, but harvest little; you eat, but there is not enough to be satisfied; you drink, but there is not enough to become drunk; you put on clothing, but no one is warm enough; and he who earns, earns wages to put into a purse with holes.'
>
> Thus says the LORD of hosts, 'Consider your ways! Go up to the mountains, bring wood and rebuild the temple, that I may be pleased with it and be glorified,' says the LORD. 'You look for much, but behold, it comes to little; when you bring it home, I blow it away. Why?' declares the LORD of hosts, 'Because of My house which lies desolate, while each of you runs to his own house. Therefore, because of you the sky has withheld its dew and the earth has withheld its produce. I called for a drought on the land, on the mountains, on the grain, on the new wine, on the oil, on what the ground produces, on men, on cattle, and on all the labor of your hands.'"
>
> —Haggai 1:4-11

I was stunned, feeling a mixture of emotions. On the positive side, I felt wonderful in that God was speaking to me and was leading me to the answer to my troubles, but I also felt my sin was being exposed. I was embarrassed, humbled, and I wanted to cry and laugh at the same time. These verses described me perfectly. I was spending all my energy trying to make money and I was angry at God for not providing as I thought He should. I was neglecting my spiritual life.

Verse 4 refers to the temple of God when it says, "My house which lies desolate." We know Jesus has changed the place of His dwelling from the temple of stone to the temple of flesh. God now dwells in our hearts, the inner man. We who know Jesus really are the temple of God. He really does dwell within and He wants us to pay first attention to our spiritual lives. I was so preoccupied with my money problems that my spiritual health was suffering greatly. God's discipline is so loving. He simply would not let me succeed when I was going in the wrong direction.

Jesus said, "But seek first His kingdom and His righteousness, and all these things will be added to you" (Matthew 6:33). Often when financial troubles begin to happen, we turn our attention away from God to solve them. In doing this, we guarantee the problem is going to eat us alive, because we come under the curse. We have the devourer on our heels, and negative things begin to happen. Most of us like to talk about spiritual miracles as positive events, but these instances are spiritual miracles in the negative: miraculous, supernatural happenings that take away our money. God has not only told us what has happened, but why it has happened. It has happened because our attention and energies are not on spiritual matters.

Another shocking verse is Joel 2:25:

> "Then I will make up to you for the years that the swarming
> locust has eaten, the creeping locust, the stripping locust, and
> the gnawing locust, My great army which I sent among you."

Two things need to grab our attention in this verse. God says the army that took away our wealth was His great army. God sent them to bring discipline into our lives.

God also says He will make up to us for the years that His army has eaten. The conditions under which He makes up to us for the years that the locust has eaten are recorded in 2 Chronicles 7:13-14:

> "If I shut up the heavens so that there is no rain, or if I command the locust to devour the land, or if I send pestilence among My people, and My people who are called by My name humble themselves and pray and seek My face and turn from their wicked ways, then I will hear from heaven, will forgive their sin and will heal their land."

The remedy is so simple. It is a three-step process:

1. We agree with God when He shows us what is wrong.
2. We talk to Him about it as we confess our sin and seek His face, not His hand.
3. We turn from our wicked ways.

When we do these things the healing will be complete.

The following Scripture references will help you begin to understand what financial bondage is all about.

- Proverbs 23:4-5 says, "Do not weary yourself to gain wealth, cease from your consideration of it. When you set your eyes on it, it is gone. For wealth certainly makes itself wings like an eagle that flies toward the heavens."
- Proverbs 28:20 says, "A faithful man will abound with blessings, but he who makes haste to be rich will not go unpunished."

These verses have to do with the person who sets his eyes on wealth and goes after it. In financial bondage, we find ourselves living under a curse. Being under a curse means God Himself has assigned to us the devourer. This is fearful stuff, but we must at least pause long enough to consider whether or not we are in financial bondage.

- "'If you do not listen and if you do not take it to heart to give honor to My name,' says the LORD of Hosts, 'then I will send the curse upon you and I will curse your blessings; and indeed, I have cursed them already, because you are not taking it to heart. Behold, I am going to rebuke your offspring, and I will spread refuse on your faces, the refuse of your feasts; and you will be taken away with it'" (Malachi 2:2-3).

  God is saying to His people, both to Israel and to us, that He will replace peace with sorrow, joy with misery, and provision with lack. Problems will arise where there were none. God simply turns our blessings upside down, but He is more than willing to make it all up to us when we repent in faith and come back to Him in that sweet intimacy that only the Holy Spirit can produce.
- "But those who want to get rich fall into temptation and a snare and many foolish and harmful desires which plunge men into ruin and destruction. For the love of money is a root of all sorts of evil, and some by longing for it have wandered away from the faith and pierced themselves with many griefs" (1 Timothy 6:9-10).

  Notice this important truth: money is not evil, but the love of it is. We do two things to ourselves when we long for money. We wander away from our faith, and we pierce ourselves with many sorrows. Faith requires that we see ourselves as belonging to God, we have been bought with the blood of Jesus Christ and we have become the temple of the Holy Spirit.

- "Do you not know that you are a temple of God, and that the Spirit of God dwells in you? If any man destroys the temple of God, God will destroy him, for the temple of God is holy, and that is what you are" (1 Corinthians 3:16-17).

We are His and everything we have is His. By loving money, we turn from Him to ourselves and entertain desires that are not of God; in fact, they are contrary to God.

- "But each one is tempted when he is carried away and enticed by his own lust. Then when lust has conceived, it gives birth to sin; and when sin is accomplished, it brings forth death" (James 1:14-15).

Paul the apostle tells us in Romans 6 that we become slaves or captives of the one we obey. "Do you not know that when you present yourselves to someone as slaves for obedience, you are slaves of the one whom you obey, either of sin resulting in death, or of obedience resulting in righteousness?" (Romans 6:16).

Thus the term *spiritual bondage* applies—when we turn to money, we become captives or slaves to money. We become bound up by the cords of our own sin.

- "His own iniquities will capture the wicked, and he will be held with the cords of his sin" (Proverbs 5:22).

God will not just turn us loose. We belong to Him forever and He will bring us back. He will discipline us as a father because that is what He is, our Heavenly Father. He does not discipline those who are not His children, but if you know Jesus as your Savior, you are God's child and He will discipline you. It is wonderful because the end result will be to make us like Jesus.

- "And you have forgotten the exhortation which is addressed to you as sons, 'My son, do not regard lightly the discipline of the LORD, nor faint when you are reproved by Him; For those whom the LORD loves He disciplines, and He scourges every son whom He receives.' It is for discipline that you endure; God deals with you as with sons; for what son is there whom his father does not discipline? But if you are without discipline, of which all have become partakers, then you are illegitimate children and not sons" (Hebrews 12:5-8).

Finally we come to the most wonderful part. *Financial freedom is a spiritual matter.* Financial freedom is only a minor part of what it means to be spiritually free. Financial freedom does not mean having lots of money; it means not having money in your heart. It means loving God with all your heart, mind, strength, and your whole being. It means knowing in your heart that God provides money and everything else because you are His beloved. The result is total contentment, total peace, and joy unspeakable. The pressure is gone, the fear is gone, the frustration is gone, and the craving for money and things money will buy is gone. Jesus said in John 8:32, "And ye shall know the truth, and the truth shall make you free" (KJV).

The truth is that we are His beloved children, His bride, His body. He loves us supremely and our greatest good is His greatest desire. He really is our Provider, and He has promised not only to meet our needs but to give us the desire of our heart. He has promised to rebuke the devourer for our sake. He has promised to open heaven's windows and pour out for us blessings so great we are not able to receive them, according to His riches in glory. He has promised to bless everything we put our hand to, and to bless every person around us, beginning with our own household. He is our Provider, our Healer, our Protector, our Wisdom, and in Him we live and move and have our being. Being free means we hear His voice, and His will about everything is not hidden from us. We are filled with such faith and confidence. We are able to see things through His eyes, and we are not influenced by the scare tactics of the world or the devil because we know that everything is in His control. If we know this truth in our hearts, we will not worry about money or anything else.

Financial troubles are not our troubles—they are God's. He takes over and turns around situations that look like troubles to us and makes great big blessings out of them. My personal experience may be of some help, although God may deal with each person differently. God looks into our hearts and works in our lives according to what we each need to draw us into full fellowship with Him.

Melinda and I were set free on July 10, 1987. We call it "being set free" for want of a better term. It was when God picked us up and loved the world out of us. It was returning to our first love. It was being restored to sweet intimacy with Jesus. It was a personal experience with the Holy Spirit where He became real and in control of our thoughts and feelings. I could go on and on about what happened that day, but I think no words can describe it.

Things did not change financially for us immediately—they got worse. From July 10, 1987 until February 1988, our financial situation deteriorated even more, but we had been set free, and a peace—even a joy—filled our hearts. The Holy Spirit spoke to my heart, saying the problem was not mine, but His, and that He would change it in His good time. I was only to cling to Him and trust that He was in complete control.

The disasters we had come to expect stopped happening, and He seemed to protect us from the collectors. He told me in my heart to be faithful in this stage because blessings were coming. Then in February, 1988, things changed. God began to pour out money from everywhere. He increased us about one thousand dollars a day for some time thereafter. Most of the increases came from totally unexpected sources.

For us, God's deliverance came in stages. First, He rebuked the devourer, in that the bad things stopped happening. Second was like the miracle of loaves and fishes—He made little cover a great need. During this time, God wanted to show me that He had taken the cares of money out of my heart, and being set free has little to do with changing the circumstances. Third was the miracle of increase, when God began to bless everything we touched. God has totally captured my heart and taught me the truth found in Deuteronomy 8:3: "Man does not live by bread alone, but man lives by everything that proceeds out of the mouth of the LORD."

When we are spiritually free, we are under the blessing and not under the curse. Romans 8:31-32 assures us,

"What then shall we say to these things? If God is for us, who is against us? He who did not spare His own Son, but delivered Him over for us all, how will He not also with Him freely give us all things?"

I have already quoted parts of the following passage from Deuteronomy 28:1-13. The entire section is key to understanding obedience in regard to finances and possessions and the resulting blessings that God will rain upon us:

"Now it shall be, if you diligently obey the LORD your God, being careful to do all His commandments which I command you today, the LORD your God will set you high above all the nations of the earth. All these blessings will come upon you and overtake you if you obey the LORD your God. Blessed shall you be in the city, and blessed shall you be in the country. Blessed shall be the offspring of your body and the produce of your ground and the offspring of your beasts, the increase of your herd and the young of your flock. Blessed shall be your basket and your kneading bowl. Blessed shall you be when you come in, and blessed shall you be when you go out. The LORD shall cause your enemies who rise up against you to be defeated before you; they will come out against you one way and will flee before you seven ways. The LORD will command the blessing upon you in your barns and in all that you put your hand to, and He will bless you in the land which the LORD your God gives you. The LORD will establish you as a holy people to Himself, as He swore to you, if you keep the commandments of the LORD your God and walk in His ways. So all the peoples of the earth will see that you are called by the name of the LORD, and they will be afraid of you. The LORD will make you abound in prosperity, in the offspring of your body and in the offspring of your beast and in the produce of your ground, in the land which the LORD swore to your fathers to give you. The LORD will open for you His good storehouse, the heavens, to give rain to your land in its season and to bless all the work of your hand; and you shall lend to many nations, but you shall not borrow. The LORD will make you the head and not the tail, and you only will be above, and you will not be underneath, if you listen to the commandments of the LORD your God, which I charge you today, to observe them carefully."

These blessings were God's promises to Israel as they entered the Promised Land, but they certainly have their counterpart for the Christian who puts God first and is led by the Holy Spirit in everything. I believe that all of God's promises found in His Word are ours and have their application in our lives.

Following are a few of the abundance of blessings available to us. I challenge you to search God's Word continually to find His promises and claim them for yourself:

- [I promise] "To endow those who love me with wealth, That I may fill their treasuries" (Proverbs 8:21).
- "It is the blessing of the LORD that makes rich, and He adds no sorrow to it" (Proverbs 10:22).
- "The generous man will be prosperous, and he who waters will himself be watered" (Proverbs 11:25).
- "Adversity pursues sinners, but the righteous will be rewarded with prosperity. A good man leaves an inheritance to his children's children, and the wealth of the sinner is stored up for the righteous" (Proverbs 13:21-22).

- "There is precious treasure and oil in the dwelling of the wise, but a foolish man swallows it up" (Proverbs 21:20).
- "The reward of humility and the fear of the LORD are riches, honor and life" (Proverbs 22:4).
- "'Bring the whole tithe into the storehouse, so that there may be food in My house, and test Me now in this,' says the LORD of hosts, 'if I will not open for you the windows of heaven and pour out for you a blessing until it overflows. Then I will rebuke the devourer for you, so that it will not destroy the fruits of the ground; nor will your vine in the field cast its grapes,' says the LORD of hosts. 'All the nations will call you blessed, for you shall be a delightful land,' says the LORD of hosts" (Malachi 3:10-12).
- "And God is able to make all grace abound to you, so that always having all sufficiency in everything, you may have an abundance for every good deed" (2 Corinthians 9:8).
- "Now to Him who is able to do far more abundantly beyond all that we ask or think, according to the power that works within us" (Ephesians 3:20).
- "But seek first His kingdom and His righteousness; and all these things will be added to you" (Matthew 6:33).
- "And He said to them, 'Truly I say to you, there is no one who has left house or wife or brothers or parents or children, for the sake of the kingdom of God, who will not receive many times as much at this time and in the age to come, eternal life'" (Luke 18:29-30).

As I conclude this biblical guide to finances, I leave you with a partial list of what God has promised if you will only walk close to Him.

- God has great plans for you (Jeremiah 29:11-14).
- God will make a little cover great needs (Matthew 14:13-21).
- God rebukes the devourer (Malachi 3:11).
- God pours out riches without sorrow (Proverbs 10:22).
- God causes the wealth of the wicked to be laid up for the righteous (Proverbs 13:22).
- God restores the years that have been wasted (Joel 2:25).
- God will give to you even in your sleep (Psalm 127:2).
- God will cause men to give to you (Luke 6:38).
- God will bless everything you put your hand to (Deuteronomy 28:8 & 12, 15:10).
- God blesses all your surroundings (Ezekiel 34:26).
- God will bless your children (Isaiah 65:23).
- God promises never to put you to shame or famine again (Ezekiel 34:29 and 36:27-29).
- God will make you the head and not the tail (Deuteronomy 28:13).
- God will bless you in all your work and undertakings (Deuteronomy 15:10).
- God promises to rain down showers of blessings (Ezekiel 34:26).
- God promises you will be the lender and not the borrower (Deuteronomy 28:12).

Go forth in anticipation of the joy and blessings that await you when you turn every aspect of your life over to God!

CPSIA information can be obtained at www.ICGtesting.com
Printed in the USA
LVOW040006131112

306946LV00004B/1/P